How to Find a Wolf in Siberia

or, How to Troubleshoot Practically Anything

Don Jones

How to Find a Wolf in Siberia

or, How to Troubleshoot Practically Anything

Don Jones

ISBN 9781720156406

Also By Don Jones

The DSC Book

The PowerShell Scripting and Toolmaking Book

Become Hardcore Extreme Black Belt PowerShell Ninja Rockstar

Be the Master

Don Jones' PowerShell 4N00bs

Don Jones' The Cloud 4N00bs

Instructional Design for Mortals

Tales of the Icelandic Troll

PowerShell by Mistake

The Culture of Learning

Contents

Part 2: The Dozen Parts of a Troubleshooting Mind

Part 3: Storytime

Introduction

"Hi there, this is [redacted], how can I help you?"

"Seems my television isn't working. It's just displaying a bright blue screen."

"Okay, I'll try and help you with that! Can you check and make sure it's plugged in?"

Pause. "Into the wall?"

"That's right, there should be a cord coming out of the electrical socket in the wall."

"Yeah, I know what electricity is. Did I mention that it's showing a bright blue screen? Like, it's clearly powered up."

"Sure, but we need to check the electrical cord."

"I'll go now, thanks."

Click. Redial.

"Hi there, this is [redacted], how can I help you?"

"Seems my television isn't working. It's just displaying a bright blue screen."

"Okay, I'll try and help you with that! Can you turn off all the circuit breakers in your house, and then turn them back on?"

Click.

We've all had calls like that, and I sure hope you've not been the circuit-breaker technician on one of them! Troubleshooting things sometimes seems like a mysterious dark art, available only to those with special aptitudes. Kind of like a wizard. And it's true that really experienced people can make troubleshooting *seem* like magic, because they've done it so many times that they run through a lot of steps in their heads. There are also natural "logical thinkers" who pick up troubleshooting a little quicker, and it's a little easier for them. But *anyone* can learn to be a better troubleshooter, and that's what this book is all about.

Troubleshooting is *not* an art. It's a science. Art stuff—painting, singing, whatever—usually does require some innate talent, along with tons of practice. Troubleshooting, technically, requires neither talent nor practice, although practice does make it go faster and smoother over time. Troubleshooting is something anyone can potentially do, so long as they possess three important personality traits:

- **Patience**. You can troubleshoot quickly, but only with practice. Troubleshooting is methodical, which means you can't skip steps, which means sometimes it takes a while. That can make it hard to remain patient when someone is screaming at you about whatever you're troubleshooting, but you need to remain calm and logical—almost Vulcan-like—in order to stay in the Zen Zone of Troubleshooting Nirvana.
- **Bravery**. Most of us don't like to fail, especially in front of other people. But troubleshooting is all about coming up with a theory, and then either proving or disproving it, and you're going to be *disproving* a lot more theories than you prove. So you're going to look like you're "failing" a lot. It's part of the process, and you can't skip it—you have to be brave enough to get through it.
- **Obsessiveness**. Troubleshooting requires a very consistent, methodical approach. You gotta do it the same way, every time, although sometimes you'll develop the odd shortcut or two. But you need to obsess about the methodology, and the process. You can't *skip* things. You often have to document a lot, and you need to be compulsive about that to make it all work out.

If all that sounds like it could be you, then you're in the right place.

I wrote this book because, aside from the materials at Troubleshooters.com (which don't really "speak" to me, personally), I wasn't finding a lot of good books on "how to troubleshoot." I think that troubleshooting is one of those skills that, once you develop it, truly elevates you above the rest of the pack. It's been a core mover-and-shaker in my own career, and a someone who loves teaching, it's something I wanted to try and express in my own words and share.

I always welcome feedback. You can use the "Hit Me Up" (HMU) link on my own site, DonJones.com.

Acknowledgements

I've used the "wolf in Siberia" analogy before, but I got it from Gil Kirkpatrick while he was at NetPro (although I can find zero instances of him using it online). He's a great guy, and *really* grasps the Troubleshooting Mind.

Part 1: The Short Version

Start here: in just 10 short "chapters," I'll walk you through the basic methodology, and give you some great tips for staying efficient and on-track.

In Part 2, we'll dig into some of these a bit more, and provide some broader context and background, but for now let's focus on the core tenets.

How do You Find a Wolf in Siberia?

Siberia is a vast, not-quite-entirely-charted territory. It has an enormous variety of terrains, and in the winter can be quite challenging to exist in. So how do you find one lone wolf in all that space?

Simple: you build a wolf-proof fence down the middle of it, and then just figure out, through some kind of test (maybe a *Star Trek*-style sensor sweep) which side the wolf is on. Once you know, you repeat the process, building a wolf-proof fence down the middle of that side, and figuring out which side the wolf is on. You repeat until you've boxed the critter in and can see him with your own eyes. The wolf-proof part is important, because it keeps him boxed in—once you eliminate a chunk of land, yo udon't need to go back and consider that chunk again.

> Another way to think about it: build a wolf-proof fence down half the territory, and listen to which side the howling is coming from. Repeat.

Now, this isn't the only troubleshooting approach in the world. There are others. But for me, this is the one that's the most broadly applicable, and useful, in almost any situation. The "wolf-proof fence" is simply a test that you run, which can eliminate one or more root causes of whatever problem you're dealing with. In reality, your "fence" might not eliminate exactly half the root causes at once, as the analogy implies, but the goal is to *definitively* eliminate one or more causes with each test you run.

Suppose you have two cars, and one morning, one won't start. So as a test, you try to start the other car, and it does start. What possible problem causes have you eliminated? *None.* No realistic ones, anyway. Your first car could still have a variety of problems: it could be out of case, have a dead battery, have a bad wire someplace, or any number of likely causes. But your test didn't eliminate any of those, and so your test was useless. A waste of time–you didn't build a wolf-proof fence.

That's the kind of "troubleshooting" I see *far* too many people engage in, particularly in my field of information technology. They waste effort, sometimes because they simply get flustered and are in a hurry, other times because they don't actually know anything about the system they're trying to test. Either way, they try more or less random stuff, or they try stuff that's worked before without knowing *why* it worked before. They burn a lot of time, sometimes feel bad about not being able to solve the problem, and perhaps worry about the security of their job.

My methodology is simple, and it isn't unique; it is–perhaps using different words–the same troubleshooting methodology you'll see taught in plenty of places. But it's incredibly effective.

1. Understand the symptoms.
2. Understand the scope.
3. Replicate the problem.
4. Divide and conquer.

Along the way, you'll need to avoid some common red herrings, like relying too much on *belief* and not entirely on *facts*, conducting inconclusive tests, and changing too many variables at one time. There are some semi-red-herrings, too, like asking, "what changed?" You'll need to pick up a little "disguised scientific method," and really train yourself to be consistent and objective. But you *can* do it.

Ready?

Before You Start: Be Cool, and Get a Notebook

Your first step is to make sure you have something to take notes with. A notepad, a copy of Microsoft OneNote, a copy of Evernote, whatever you prefer. You're going to be taking a lot of notes. A *lot*. And if you're the type who doesn't like to take notes (I am), you need to get over it. Troubleshooting, as I've already written, is *science*. That makes you a *scientist*, and scientists keep notes. After all, if you forget which bits of Siberia you've already ruled out, you're likely to waste time going back to them.

Seriously, if this step is one you're going to try and skip, then just stop reading right here.

 I'll use this icon to specifically call out the things you need to take notes on.

This is also the time to be cool. Don't be stressed. Don't be worried. Be calm, collected, and analytical. Get your scientist brain booted up and working. Ignore outside distractions and pressures. Work efficiently, but not messily. You don't need your brain flooded with adrenaline and panic as you begin troubleshooting; you need it focused on the task at hand.

Remember:

1. You can do this.
2. You can't do this if you're not going to be cool, logical, and methodical about it. Think Spock. Be Spock.
3. Spock can do this.
4. You can *do* this.

Understand the Symptoms

Make sure you really understand the symptoms of the problem, and make sure you understand them in *the greatest detail possible*. My own Beloved Spouse will often complain that something went wrong on the iPad, and when I ask, "well, was there any kind of message?" it's always, "yeah, but I forgot it." You *need* that information in order to troubleshoot.

"Oh, the iPad shut down suddenly."

"Was there any kind of message?"

"Yeah, it said something about installing an update."

"OK, keep an eye on it and call me back in ten minutes."

In this case, the *full symptom description* told an experienced person that this problem would go away on its own after the iPad rebooted.

Write down the symptoms in your notebook. Write down every detail you're given. I try to put each distinct detail on a separate line, because each one is a piece of evidence in the crime I'm solving. Having them separated a bit, visually, makes it easier for me to take each one into account.

As you gain experience in working with a system, you'll be able to ask better qualifying questions to reveal more symptoms. Even if you're the one experiencing the problem, it's good to run through some questions and just try and draw some more detail out of the situation.

"The smart lock on the front door isn't unlocking."

- "Did the keypad beep when you were punching in the code?"
- "Did you notice if the lights came on?"
- "Did it make that motor sound that it does when it's unlocking?"
- "Were you leaning against the door at the time?"

Some of these questions are designed to better clarify the *situation* than the problem *per se.* "What were you doing when it happened?" is a good generic question, along with variations like, "what did you do right before it all went wrong?" You're not blaming the problem on the person you're speaking to–and it can be important to emphasize that with them–you're trying to understand the *situation.* Problems are very often situational, like the car that starts fine when it's warm, but won't start when it's freezing outside.

 Again, make notes of every detail about the situation that you can.

As you ask your clarifying questions, it's important to stay on-track. This gets easier as you gain experience with whatever it is you're troubleshooting. You don't, for example, want to ask questions like, "do you always wear that color shirt?" when you're troubleshooting someone's broken microwave. Common-sensically, the two are definitely unrelated. When you're new with something, there can be a sort of instinct to ask too few questions, just so you don't start straying into things that–without you realizing it–have no bearing on the topic. That's okay–again, as you gain experience, you'll "hone in" a little better.

Better understanding the symptoms is just *so* crucial. I mean, if you're looking for a wolf in Siberia when one has been killing livestock in Canada, you're going to be wasting your time, right?

Understand the Scope

Scope refers, you might say, to the *size* of a problem.

"This apple is rotten."

"What about the other apples?"

In many troubleshooting situations, you're not dealing with one unique thing, so it's worth looking into whether or not other similar, or exactly-alike things, are also experiencing the same problem.

"My laptop isn't getting anything from the Internet."

"Does you sister's laptop have Internet?"

The important thing is to ask questions that have *commonality*. In that brief example, "access to the Internet" was the putative problem, and so figuring out if another device on the same network was having the same problem would be revealing. It'd be a good wolf-proof fence: if the sister's laptop isn't working either, then the odds are there's a problem with the home network or with the service provider. On the other hand, if Sissy's laptop *is* working, then the problem is almost definitely with the problematic laptop, and not with the network or the service provider.

"My car won't start."

"Did you try starting the other car?"

That's perhaps a bad scoping question, because what possible common thread could cause two cars to not start? Sure, they could both be suffering from the *same problem*, like a lack of fuel, but they'd be suffering independently, not from a *common* lack of fuel. Even if you're thinking, "well, maybe they're both freezing cold," it's not a good scoping question, because it's unlikely two cars–even of the same model–would have the exact same reaction at the same time, for the same reason. Scoping questions are designed around *commonality*, and they're intended as a first step in building wolf-proof fences. The answer to a scoping question should help narrow the problem down to the specific thing experiencing a problem, or to the broader system that two things share.

Be *really* wary of leaping to conclusions.

"Hey, my laptop isn't connecting to this website."

"Oh, no problem, I'll just reboot the router."

Whoa! You didn't even ask if they'd opened a web browser! You didn't ask if they could connect to a different website! You're already taking down the entire network as a solution? Sure, they may have worked for some problem in the past, but who's to say this is the same root cause? You haven't done any actual troubleshooting yet, so it's too soon to be taking action, especially when those actions might create even more negative impact.

Write down your scope observations. What other things are affected by the same problem? What things aren't? What are the common threads that are working, and the common threads that aren't?

Scope is a component of the problem's symptoms, in many ways. I find that a good way to make sure I'm accurately assessing scope is to rely on three of the Ws:

- **When** does the problem happen? All the time, or only when you do certain things? Only at certain times of the day?

- **Where** does the problem show up? Are you always in the same place doing the same thing, or does it crop up in multiple spots? Does it affect a group of similar things, or just one thing?
- **Who** does the problem affect? For example, if Marty's card key doesn't work on a certain door but Jim's does, then the door itself probably isn't to fault.

Replicate the Problem

Once you've got the problem described and scoped, you need to try and recreate it. Sometimes this is easy:

 "The TV won't come on."

"Let me try. Yup, you're right."

Other times, it can be far more complicated, and take more time. The thing is, though, that you can't really properly troubleshoot something that you can't replicate. Troubleshooting is going to involve testing things–building your wolf-proof fences–and you can't do that unless you've got a broken thing to test against. *Intermittent problems*, or ones that only seem to occur when you're not personally looking, are the very devil of the troubleshooting world. The most you can often do with them is go back to "Understand the Symptoms" and try to collect more information. Is there any common thread to when the problem occurs?

A real thing that happened to me: we had an outside patio electric outlet that would intermittently fail. We'd plugged a lamp into it, and the lamp would sometimes come on, and sometimes not. It wasn't those stupid GFCI outlets; since we'd been unable to replicate the problem consistently, and since those suckers tend to be a failure point, I'd already replaced them. No help. Which goes to show you the costs and time involved in "fixing" something where you don't have the root cause. There *was*, it turned out, a common situational thread: when we sat outside at night, and tried to use that lamp, we *usually* had the master bathroom overhead light turned off. It wasn't until one of us went inside one evening to use the bathroom, turned on the light, and the outside lamp came on, that we realize the outlet had been wired *off that same switch* for some insane reason. I pulled the switch apart and rewired it, and all was well.

So replicating the problem *can* be difficult sometimes, but know that without being able to do so, you're basically taking shots in the dark with any fixes you try. You're trying stuff that *may* work, and possibly *should* work, but might still *not* work.

Replicating the problem requires you to truly *replicate* the problem. You need to be comparing apples to apples, and sometimes that's hard to do. Spouse's laptop can't get to the Internet, kid's laptop can't get to the Internet, *your* laptop gets to the Internet just fine. So now instead of truly troubleshooting the problem, you're kind of on a tangent of, "well, what's different with *my* machine, then?" You've not *replicated* the problem, although you're certainly able to test-and-troubleshoot on one of the affected laptops. You've asked a good scoping question, and you may have a decent wolf-proof fence, right? I mean, the problem is clearly not your home network, because *your* laptop works, right?

Wrong. You haven't replicated the problem, and so you haven't built a wolf-proof fence. For example, maybe *your* laptop works because it's connected to the neighbor's network, something you set up when you were over there helping them install their new home theater system. You're using a different network, and so "test results" ("mine works!") from your system aren't valid in diagnosing or scoping the problem. You've built a wolf-proof fence in an entirely different country, and it won't help you find the wolf in Siberia.

Prerequisite: Know the System

And log what you don't know. Be able to map the system you're testing, if a map isn't provided to you. Beware of abstractions.

Your next step–and this isn't a "step" so much as something you have to have in advance–is to truly *know* whatever it is you're troubleshooting. Like, when you start the car, *what actually happens?* You need to beware of *abstractions*, here–things that sit "on top" of whatever the actual system is, hiding its details from you. Perhaps you think you start the car by plopping in the seat, pressing the brake, and pressing the "on" button while the key fob is in your pocket? That's an abstraction, and it's hiding much of the real detail from you.

In some cases, whatever you're troubleshooting may have a service manual that includes flowcharts, which describe how the system really works. Sometimes, those manuals will even have troubleshooting flowcharts, which guide you through the process and instruct you to take specific tests to discover the root cause of the problem. And, sometimes, you're just on your own.

If you don't know the system, then you can't test the system, and you can't troubleshoot the system. If you don't know that a car uses fuel, then you won't know to check the fuel gauge. If you don't realize that *this* particular car is all-electric, and needs to be plugged in and not filled up, then you can't troubleshoot "the car won't start." This doesn't mean you need to be an expert: I'm not an auto mechanic, but I can still do a decent amount of basic troubleshooting using simple tools like my eyes and ears. I know a *tiny* bit about how the car works, and that's enough to take me surprisingly far in my troubleshooting.

Start by testing your knowledge, beginning with the point of the problem. "When I flip the light switch, the light won't come on." Okay, what *normally* happens when you flip the light switch? The answer is not, "the light comes on;" there's a bit more happening behind the scenes. If you don't know what that is, *no problem.* Write down what it is you don't know.

 This is where we're back to your notebook. Seriously, *write down* what you don't know, because that's going to become a learning list.

In fact, when you flip a normal light switch, a metal blade swings up between two electrical contacts. That completes a circuit, and the light goes on. Knowing that brings up more potential problems, right? In addition to the power simply being off, or a wire being loose, or the bulb being burned out, you could have a bad switch. It could be gummed up with dust, for example, preventing a circuit from being completed. Or the interior blade could be broken, so nothing's actually happening when you flip the plastic toggle switch. The point is that *knowing how the system works* is crucial to being able to test it.

Documenting *what you don't know* is crucial to being able to *go learn.* Google is your friend, here, if you don't have a suitable manual for whatever system you're troubleshooting. Go find out how it works, in as much detail as you can. Yes, this will take time– but it's *invested* time. The time you invest now will pay back later, because you'll be able to troubleshoot that system much faster once you know how it works.

You can't go on until you know how the system works. So solve that, and then continue. Learn how the system is supposed to work, whether that means reading up on it or something else.

Not surprisingly, a self-perceived lack of knowledge is why most people get a little panicky when they're asked to troubleshoot something. But *nobody knows everything.* Anyone who's ever done any troubleshooting ever has probably *learned something new while doing it.* So you should *expect* to not have every answer going in. What you need to have confidence in is *your ability to learn as you go.* Most human learning occurs "just in time," in your moment of need, not in classes you took or books you read. So long as you're a diligent researcher, and you're not afraid to learn on-the-fly, you'll be fine. However, if you're thinking, "I can't possibly troubleshoot anything unless I know everything about it up front," then you're probably right—you can't possibly troubleshoot anything.

A lack of knowledge is something you can fix. Don't be afraid or get flustered because you don't currently know; you *will* know, once you teach yourself. Don't ask questions like, "how do I fix this?" Instead, ask questions like, "how does this work when it's not broken?" That's a question that reflects the right mindset.

Fish vs. Fishing

I spend a lot of time answering technical questions in online Q&A forums. One of the things that frustrates me the most is when people come looking for the *wrong answer.*

Here's what I mean by that. If you're trying to accomplish something, whether it's building something new or fixing something broken, the *right answer* is understanding how that think should work. The *wrong answer* is whatever will make your current problem go away.

In other words, don't ask me how to fix your problem. That's *your* job. Ask me *how should this work in the first place?* That's an effort to teach yourself, to make yourself more knowledgeable, and it's a question I and others can respect and try to help with. The upside is that, once you know how something works, you'll not only be better equipped to fix your current problem, you'll be better equipped to avoid and fix future problems as well.

When something is broken, I don't want to just hand you a fish, because the next time something breaks you'll be hungry again. I acknowledge that being a pretty tortured analogy. When you've got something broken, I want to *teach you to fish*, so that you can self-help the next time. That's really what this book is all about–you just need the right attitude.

Test

Before we get started, I want to come clean. I've titled this book using an analogy for the "divide and conquer" process of troubleshooting, and that is indeed a process I'm often able to use. But sometimes you can't. Sometimes, you have to take a more methodical approach, testing each step of a system's process until you find a problem. For me, the difference between "top-down," "bottom-up," and "divide-and-conquer" troubleshooting is entirely moot. They all require an understanding of the system being tested, and they all require you to perform tests. The only difference, when you really get right down to the nuts and bolts of it all, is that sometimes your tests eliminate a vast swath of potential problems, and other times they only eliminate one. Either way, you're building wolf-proof fences; it's just sometimes, you're building them down the middle of the country, and sometimes you're just starting really close to one border. So long as each fence definitively rules out some chunk of the terrain, you're doing your job.

Regardless, now it's time to start testing. There's really only one rule for a troubleshooting test: it needs to *definitively* confirm or eliminate one or more possible causes of the problem.

 "Hon, the smart door lock isn't locking."

"OK, I'll replace the battery."

Is that a good troubleshooting step? Not really. It's an attempt at a fix. Yes, replacing the battery should definitively prove that the battery either was, or was not, the cause of the problem. But perhaps poking the keypad to see if it beeped could have done that, without a potentially wasted replacement. You've taken a shortcut, and a potentially "expensive" one compared to just poking the keypad.

"Hey, the air conditioner isn't coming on."

"Does the digital thermostat say anything?"

"No, it's completely blank."

"I'll check the circuit breaker."

That was a decent start to troubleshooting. You knew that the air conditioner system requires power, and that if it has power, the thermostat would display something. Since it isn't, you've developed a theory that the power must be out. The circuit breaker is likely the next up-the-line cause for a lack of power, so it makes sense to check it. Your first test–checking the thermostat display–was a good wolf-proof fence. You've eliminated an entire wedge of potential, "you have the thermostat set wrong" problems, because you know the thermostat isn't even on. The circuit breaker isn't necessarily the cause; the thermostat could be getting power, but could be burned out or otherwise nonfunctional, requiring replacement. But the breaker is a cheap and easy test to perform, so it makes sense to do that next.

Knowing the system is key, although being an *expert* isn't. For example, when you direct your computer's web browser to a website, *what does it do?* What can you test to see if each step in the process is working or not? The computer contacts its Domain Name Service (DNS) server to translate the website name into a numerical address. This requires the computer to go out to the Internet-based DNS server; you could manually test this *name resolution* using a low-level utility like Ping. If the ping is able to resolve the name, then you've eliminated a pretty big set of potential problems: you know your Internet connection is live, you know the website address is correctly spelled, and you know that the DNS system is able to provide a numerical address. It's a good first test, but you wouldn't know about it unless you knew how the system worked in the first place.

Some tests are only good at testing one "side" of the problem–that is, confirming the problem or eliminating the problem–but not both. Take the same, "I can't get to this website" problem. One test might be to use the same computer, but a different web browser. If that test gets you to the website, then you've confirmed that the original web browser was the problem somehow. But, if the test *doesn't* get you to the website, then you've really not eliminated anything. *Both* browsers could be screwed up somehow, and you've not really eliminated any other possible problems. Try to perform tests that either *positively confirm a problem* or *positively eliminate a problem* either way; avoid tests that can only do one or the other.

Let's explore that further.

The Scientific Method and Troubleshooting

Troubleshooting is an application of the Scientific Method. Basically the Scientific Method requires you to state a theory or hypothesis, and then conduct experiments to either prove or disprove it.

 "Honey, the pool pump isn't running."

THEORY: The pool pump has no power.
EXPERIMENT: Check the circuit breaker.
RESULT: Breaker is on. THEORY FAILED.
EXPERIMENT: Use a voltage meter to check the meter at the pump.
RESULT: Correct voltage applied to pump. THEORY FAILED.

THEORY: The pump is frozen.
EXPERIMENT: Use a wrench to try and manually unfreeze the pump.
RESULT: Turns freely but still not running. THEORY FAILED.

THEORY: Spouse pushed pump button on inside control panel.
EXPERIMENT: Push pump button.
RESULT: Pump running. THEORY CONFIRMED.

Yeah, probably should have checked that last one first, right? Occam's Razor: the simplest explanation is probably the right one. But this thought process is a good one: each time, a theory is proposed, and an experiment conducted that will definitively prove or disprove *just that theory*.

This is where it's good to write down what you're testing and, more importantly, *why* you're testing it. When I'm testing an unfamiliar or very complex system, I actually do take notes, and they look a lot like the series above, with the word "THEORY" in all caps and everything.

 For each test you perform, first write down your theory. Then write down your planned test, as I did in the narrative above. Then conduct the test, and note the result.

Writing everything down is a good way to double-check yourself. What is it exactly that I hope my test will prove or disprove? Am I pretty sure that this test will definitely do one of those–prove or disprove? What's the theory, here?

 "Babe, the TV isn't turning on. The remote is dead."

"Love of my life, that same remote also turns the audio receiver on. Is it doing that?"

"Yeah, it's turning that on and off."

"So why do you think the remote is dead?"

"The TV isn't coming on."

"So what's your theory?"

[Angrily] "I don't know, maybe the TV half of the remote is dead or only one of the batteries is dead!?!?"

Funny, but if more people had this conversation with themselves– if more people asked, "hey, what's my actual theory, here?" Then they'd be more efficient troubleshooters. Trying to start car #2 when car #1 didn't start would require a pretty outrageous theory. Maybe an alien car-suppression field being broadcast over town? If you can't state a reasonable theory, then there's probably little point in doing that test. Save yourself some time, and find a *plausible* theory, and then test it. And *state* your theory. Say it aloud. Because a lot of times, just taking a 2-second pause to state your theory will help you realize if it passes the "sniff test" or not. Just letting your brain reflect on a formal theory for just a moment can also start to trigger all sorts of memory associations to help you prove or disprove the theory.

"What Changed?"

A lot of times–a *very* lot of times–when something that *was* working is not *not* working, folks will ask, "what changed?"

"What changed" is *not* troubleshooting. You are not proposing a theory (other than, "something changed," which is pretty obvious), and you can't usually run any tests to tell you what changed. Sometimes, "what changed" can *cue* some good troubleshooting.

 "Why isn't the light bulb turning on?"

"Well, I suppose the bulb could have burned out in last night's lightning storm."

That's a statement of *what changed*, but it's also a valid, testable hypothesis. You may have internally asked yourself "what changed?" but you didn't actually spend a lot of time trying to answer that question. Instead, you worked through what you knew about the system's workings, and stated a theory that you can now test.

With more complex systems, people can spend more time figuring out "what changed," and attempting to on-change it, than they might have spent just troubleshooting the actual problem. "What changed" is a *shortcut*; an alternative to troubleshooting, and when it's a question quickly answered and quickly resolved, it's a good shortcut. But it's still not troubleshooting; it's an alternate way of solving the problem. On the plus side, it often requires less knowledge of how the problem system actually works, which is a reason I suspect people kind of default to "what changed" in the first place: they don't know enough about how the system works to actually troubleshoot it, and so the "what changed" shortcut becomes their primary mechanism for resolving the problem.

I don't mean to come off as being anti-"what changed." I'm not. It *can* be a useful mechanism, especially–again–when it's a true shortcut that's quickly answered and quickly resolved. I just want you to recognize that being able to answer "what changed?" does not make you a good troubleshooter, and troubleshooting is the more valuable skill. Here's why: sometimes, "what changed" was something *intentional*. Yes, it make have broken something, but simply "undoing" the change isn't an option. In those cases, the shortcut isn't as useful for solving the problem. Troubleshooting still would be.

Control Your Variables

As you perform tests, keep in mind the need to *control your variables.* That is, you typically want to test just *one* thing, or one small group of tightly-coupled things, at a time. When a light switch doesn't work, you don't change the switch *and* pull out the wiring *and* change the bulb all in one step; you'd start with the simplest and easiest troubleshooting step, and just test one thing.

This is where it can be really important to *state your theory,* in writing, and *then* state the test that you'll use to prove or disprove the theory. Ask yourself: is my test limited to *just* my theory, or is my test much bigger than that? Am I testing too much at once?

 PROBLEM: Laptops can't get to Internet
THEORY: Home network is messed up
EXPERIMENT: Reboot all laptops, reboot home router.

This is too much. First of all, it's not a *test,* it's an *attempted repair.* It's also testing a lot of things. Now, it might fix the problem, and if your family is okay with the disruption, then maybe this is the fastest way to a resolution. But it's not *troubleshooting* at all–you're just pushing all the buttons at once. The problem may be *gone,* but it wasn't *solved.* An actual troubleshooting scenario might have looked like this:

PROBLEM: Laptops can't get to Internet
THEORY: Laptops aren't connected to router.
EXPERIMENT: Confirm laptops think they're on the network.
RESULT: They do. THEORY FAIL.
THEORY: Home router is not responding
EXPERIMENT: See if laptops can ping the home router.
RESULT: No. THEORY POSSIBLY CONFIRMED; reboot router.
RESULT: THEORY CONFIRMED, everything's fine now.

The theories are more specific, this time. Before, it was just restating the problem, really; it wasn't a theory. Here, only one thing was proposed, and one thing tested, at a time. You've only got one thing being examined, or changed, at a time, and so you can easily pin down which one worked.

This applies to attempted repairs, too. If you've got a light bulb not coming on, and you replace it but it still doesn't come on, *put the old light bulb back* and move on to the next theory, like a circuit breaker being out. If you've tested something, think you've found the problem, and then turn out to be wrong, *put it back the way it was*, unless you've confirmed through testing that whatever change you made at least made things better. Otherwise, you wind up with an accumulation of changes, and it becomes tough to put your finger on *what worked*.

It's crucial to document what you change–take pictures, if that's applicable. Record a video. Make a diagram. Whatever you can document, do so in great detail *so that you can put things back again* if needed.

Think of troubleshooting as a road. You don't have precise directions to where you're going, and so you have to experiment a bit.

Once you take a side road, if it turns out to be the wrong road, *you go back*. You undo what you've done and try again at the next side road. But you don't just keep blindly taking turns, because you'll never get to where you were going (except maybe by accident), and you'll have an increasingly hard time getting back to where you started. You'll be lost.

Part 2: The Dozen Parts of a Troubleshooting Mind

In this Part, we'll go into more depth, with more examples, and more ways of mentally approaching troubleshooting. The idea is to get you to a place where you're *always* in that logical, scientific mental space, making you a more effective troubleshooter whenever the need arises.

I've noticed, and you probably have to, that some people just seem to have a brain built for troubleshooting. They don't. They've **built** a brain for troubleshooting by focusing on a dozen key characteristics, and you can do the same thing. Their brains automatically divide and conquer using wolf-proof fences, and you can train your own mind to do the same.

Bear in mind that this Part isn't meant to be procedural; the procedure is still the one you read about in Part 1. This Part is a more nuanced look at portions of that procedure, with an eye toward making you more effective over the long-haul. Becoming a better troubleshooter is going to take some time, so this Part will also offer some advice about where to best spend that time.

As a note to my Agile Leanpub readers, I'm very much still playing with this section. I'd expect a lot of "churn" in the following chapters, and I certainly welcome your feedback via the "Email the Author" link on the book's Leanpub home page, or use the "HMU" link on DonJones.com.

00. Eschews Belief; Hungers for Facts

I have a bit of a bug about the word *belief*. We use it a lot in casual conversation, but it's a powerful word. When used correctly, it can precisely indicate your state of confidence and desire about something. For example:

1. I believe that most grass is green.
2. I believe that Santa Claus is a real person.
3. I believe that universal health insurance is a good thing.
4. I believe Saturn has more moons than currently advertised.

In #1 there, you don't *need* belief. You can demonstrably prove, using objective criteria, that the statement is true. Using the word "believe" here is incorrect. You might instead state that, "I can prove that most grass is green."

In #2, you're using "believe" the correct way. You're referring to something that you *want* to be true, but you're not really interested in having it proven or disproven. That's fine–by using the word "believe" in this case, you're indicating a lack of hard facts and your lack of concern with that lack of hard facts.

In #3, you're stating an *opinion*. It's neither provable nor disprovable, although you might be open to debate on the subject. There is no objectively right or wrong response to this statement, and "believe" is probably a vague word to use. You might instead state that, "In my opinion, universal health care is a good thing." This helps make it clearer that you're not stating a Santa Claus-style belief, but rather expressing an opinion which is not objectively right or wrong.

Finally, in #4, your belief is inappropriate. Whether or not Saturn has extra moons lurking in orbit *can* be objectively proven. Remember, *belief* implies that you're not interested in proof, or that whatever you believe in *can't* be objectively proven; the situation with Saturn's moons *can* be. It would be better to state, "I hypothesize that Saturn has more moons that currently cataloged." Making it clear that you're stating a theory also makes it clear that, while you don't currently possess facts proving or disproving your theory, you're aware that such facts could be produced in the future, and that you yourself might be interested in such facts.

In troubleshooting, only theories and facts are welcome. *Beliefs*–things you can't prove or disprove–aren't helpful. Saying, "I think the car might be out of gas" is a vague statement. Someone with a Troubleshooting Mind wouldn't be interested in vague statements. They'd say, "I theorize that the car is out of gas," and then proceed to run a test to prove or disprove their theory. In a Troubleshooting Mind, there are no beliefs or opinions; there are theories and facts.

01. Is Proactive: Has a Knowledge Base

A Troubleshooting Mind knows two things:

1. Memories are fickle.
2. People move on.

As you learn more about the systems that you are responsible for maintaining and fixing, you'll learn tons of useful facts, tips, and tricks. You'll learn more about which symptoms point to which problems, making troubleshooting (and fixing) faster. But memories are fickle. You'll misremember something eventually, and it'll slow you down or even make your situation worse. And, eventually, you're going to have to move on to something else in life, and all of your experience will go with you. This is where a Knowledge Base, or KB, comes in.

A KB serves as your auxiliary brain. It can be as simple as a Word document, although it's far more useful as a searchable database. Many companies already use KBs for technology issues, and it's easy to set up your own for whatever field you're in. For example, most doctors subscribe to KBs that help them make clinical diagnoses faster.

An ideal KB lets you write some kind of statement that describes a problem. You include a list of symptoms, and you then include a list of tests that you would run to narrow the problem down. You include information about any tools needed to run those tests. Finally, you include information about fixing the problem, depending on the outcome of the test. In some cases, these KB entries can just be written text. In other cases, you might find a flowchart to be

most useful. Sometimes, a KB entry might not contain the solution–
instead, it might walk someone through some basic troubleshooting
steps, and if those don't solve the problem then it might direct
them to escalate the problem to a more experienced person. But
the point of it all is to make it easier to search for problems that
have happened in the past, and to document how the problem can
be diagnosed and solved.

02. Knows the Symptoms in Depth

Put most people in front of a problem–and then get the boss screaming about "when'll it be fixed!"–and they tend to drop right into "fix-it mode." They'll immediately start running tests to try and narrow down the cause of the problem.

> "Hey Ben, what seems to be the problem?"
>
> "Oh Mary, thank goodness. I'm not able to get to the Internet! I've got a report due to the boss in thirty and without the Internet I can't pull the last numbers I need!"
>
> "Oh gosh, OK–let me start troubleshooting this for you!"
>
> Mary spends twenty minutes making sure Ben's computer is connected to the company network, and that it's able to access the company Internet router. She eliminates several possible causes, all while Ben gets increasingly panicked about the time. Finally, she pulls up a web browser on Ben's computer and is able to reach Google.com.
>
> "Ben, I'm not having any trouble getting to Google– what were you trying?"
>
> "I'm trying to get to this website," he says, pointing to a shortcut on his desktop. Mary opens it, and receives a "DENIED" notification from the company's security system. Ben can get to the Internet just fine, but that particular website is blocked for some reason.

See, Mary jumped right into testing mode before she really understood all of the symptoms. Troubleshooting is like detective work. If you're a good detective, and you're called to a crime scene with a dead body, your first step is just to sort of stand and take in the scene. What's been disturbed? What's laying around? You don't immediately launch a manhunt for the murderer. If you did, you'd be pretty embarrassed when the cause of death turned out to be accidental carbon monoxide poisoning, right?

The Troubleshooting Mind collects data before it starts troubleshooting. It seeks to understand the exact thing that isn't working, and then it attempts to recreate that exact thing, to be sure that it actually understands the problem's symptoms.

03. Knows its Tools

Tests are what makes troubleshooting possible. We can spew out all the theories we want on why something isn't working, but if we can't test those theories, then we can't prove or disprove them, which means we can't ultimately solve the problem in a consistent, efficient manner.

And in order to test something, you need a tool.

Sometimes a tool is as simple as a little computer program you might run to verify connectivity to something. Other times, a tool might be a physical piece of hardware that you use. Whatever the case, *all theories are useless unless you have a tool to prove or disprove them through a test.* Water heater not working? You might need an ohmmeter to test the resistance across the heating elements. Car overheating? You might need tools that can test the car's various systems, such as its sensors, pumps, and so forth.

For whatever systems you have to troubleshoot, you will need to know the tools associated with those systems, and you'll need to know them *well.* It is absolutely worth the time to learn how to use a tool completely and properly.

It is *not* sufficient just to read a troubleshooting manual which instructs you to use a tool to perform a specific test. Once you've used that tool for the first time, you need to get the manual for that tool, and learn how to use it for everything it's capable of doing. *Master* that tool. After all, if a tool was designed to test something, there's a *reason* it was designed to test that something, and then reason is probably because that something breaks from time to time. Learning to use a tool *completely* will introduce you, indirectly, to many of the problem situations that the tool can help solve. Thus, when one of those situations arises, you will be pre-equipped to better understand it, run tests, and solve it.

As you learn about a system and how it's supposed to work, constantly ask yourself–or someone else–"hey, if this bit wasn't working, how would I test it? What tools are available?"

I once worked on F-14 Tomcat aircraft, which are–even though they were designed in the 1970s–incredibly complex machines. One component of the aircraft is a hydraulic pressure module. It's designed to measure the pressure of the plane's hydraulic systems. Certain critical systems, like flight controls, always receive hydraulic fluid, no matter what the pressure; other less-critical systems only receive fluid if the system pressure is healthy. That way, if there's a problem, the critical stuff is most likely to get what it needs, even if that means shutting off less-critical things.

When my instructors were explaining this system, they explained how the pressure module worked. Essentially, the fluid goes into one end, and pushes against a valve that's connected to a spring. The valve has two outlets, one at the top, and one closer to the bottom. Fluid can always make it out the top outlet, which is then connected to the critical flight systems. In order for fluid to make it out the bottom outlet, and to the less-critical systems, the fluid pressure has to overcome that spring. Push hard enough against the valve, and the spring will compress, revealing the lower outlet for fluid. Normally, that spring is compressed all the time; it's only when pressure falls that the spring extends and shuts off the lower outlet.

You can perhaps already imagine some of the things that go wrong. Outlets might become blocked up, or the valve might not slide smoothly in its casing. So we had tools that would let us apply a specific amount of hydraulic pressure to the inlet, and then test to see which outlets were releasing fluid.

"How do we test the spring?" I asked.

"You don't need to," they said. "If fluid's coming out the lower outlet when the inlet is at the right pressure, and if fluid stops coming out when you back the pressure off, then the spring is working."

"Yes," I said, "I get that. But if it's not working, there are several things that could be wrong. I'd like to know how to test the spring, by itself."

We had to get the manual out, but it turns out the facility possessed a specific little tool to test those springs. I learned how to use it, and not surprisingly, I used it quite a bit when I was in the shop that repaired those pressure modules.

The Troubleshooting Mind seeks to know its tools, and it wants tools that isolates each possible problem cause, and lets it test each one as independently as possible.

04. Knows When "Wrong" is Right

In the first Part of this book, I pointed out some techniques that aren't technically troubleshooting.

Take "repair-as-troubleshooting" as an example. This is where you just take a kind of wild guess about what the cause of a problem might be, and actually apply a fix to that cause, without actually testing to see if it's the cause. It's not troubleshooting–but it's not *always* wrong. Many people with a practiced and honed Troubleshooting Mind develop a kind of instinct about the systems they troubleshoot, and they know that *sometimes*, it's actually easier, cheaper, faster, and/or less disruptive to just try and apply a quick, simple fix, and see if it makes the problem go away. "Did you try rebooting your computer?" is a try-the-quick-fix approach we're all familiar with, because in many instances it *does* fix the problem, and the alternative could be days of complex troubleshooting. Rebooting is usually fast, easy, and non-destructive, and while it won't actually identify the cause of the problem, when it *makes the problem go away* it's a valid technique.

Asking yourself, "what changed, here?" in response to a problem also isn't troubleshooting. But, in instances where you can quickly, easily, and cheaply figure out what has changed, and then quickly revert a change to fix a problem, it can be a legitimate approach. It's not troubleshooting: you're not conducting tests to pinpoint a root cause of a problem. Even if you find and successfully revert a change, you might still need extensive testing to understand what that change caused the problem. That testing phase is the troubleshooting bit; the "just put it back the way it was" is just a quick workaround to get things working again in the short term.

Really, when you're confronted with a problem you should have two goals in mind:

1. Understand the root cause and how to fix it.
2. Get things working again quickly.

Troubleshooting is the only way to accomplish #1. But certain not-troubleshooting things, like "repair-as-troubleshooting," the "shotgun" approach of trying several quick fixes, or "put it back the way it was" can all help achieve #2, and sometimes #2 is the more pressing goal. So it's fine to do these "wrong" things when they help you get to #2 more quickly, *provided* you still remember that #1 is also a goal. After things are back working, you still need to pin down the root cause of the problem, so that you can work toward *preventing* a recurrence in the future.

05. Knows that "Know the System" Doesn't Mean Expertise

I think one of the toughest things for newer troubleshooters to realize is that while you do need to know how a system behaves, you *don't* need to be an absolute expert in the system in order to troubleshoot it.

 My air conditioning won't come on, and I don't know anything about air conditioners!

Well, that's just not true. You know that an air conditioner requires electricity, and you know that things like circuit breakers control the flow of power. You know that the A/C unit has a thermostat, even if you don't know how a thermostat works inside. You can do *some* troubleshooting, even if you can only narrow the problem down to, "I need to call someone with more expertise." Too many people, however, just throw their hands in the air and give up before they've even really begun.

When I worked as an aircraft mechanic for the Navy (I was a civilian employee), maintenance was broken into three levels:

- Organizational maintenance was the aircraft squadron itself. The squadron mechanics simply weren't trained in super-deep levels of expertise. They mainly relied on troubleshooting flowcharts, and their main activity was to swap out malfunctioning components and modules. They needed quick-and-dirty troubleshooting and repairs, because the aircraft carrier just didn't have room for anything more complex to occur.

- Busted components would go to Intermediate maintenance, usually at a specialized shore facility. Intermediate mechanics would have more training on how specific components works, and would rework them back to specification.
- Depot level maintenance tore the entire plane down to nuts and bolts, reworked every component, and put it all back together. The level of training was much higher (my apprenticeship was four years, which is roughly how long most sailors' first enlistment runs). Notably, we didn't do a lot of troubleshooting at the Depot level, because we were more or less building an aircraft from scratch, but when we did run into problems it was usually involving multiple systems and required a lot of tools, diagnostics, and know-how.

Troubleshooting happens on multiple levels with any system, and just because you can't do Depot-level maintenance on an air conditioner doesn't mean you can't do Organizational-level troubleshooting.

 My car won't start! I'm no ASE mechanic, so I really can't do anything about it.

Again, that's just not true. The mechanic you take your car to is performing Intermediate- and Depot-level maintenance; nothing is stopping a relative neophyte from doing some Organizational-level stuff. You know the car runs on gas. You know it makes a certain noise when you start it. Does it contain gas now? What noise is it making when you try to start it? Does the battery have a charge– that's a simple test anyone can make using a $30 multimeter from the hardware store.

So much of our day-to-day lives involve handing off all responsibility for troubleshooting to someone else ("I'll just call AAA") that we start to build up a mental block around troubleshooting itself. Sure, you may not *want* to deal with your car, and that's fine, so long as you don't let yourself develop an attitude of helplessness when confronted with systems you *do* have to troubleshoot.

The Troubleshooting Mind knows a couple of important things: first, that you *can* eliminate at least a few potential problem causes. You can build at least a *few* wolf-proof fences, and eliminate at least *some* of the territory that wolf might be in. Maybe you can't find the damn critter, but you can certainly narrow it down. Second, the Troubleshooting Mind also knows that it can *learn*. Even if you can't proactively learn enough to solve your problem, and you have to refer the problem to someone with more system expertise, you can still *ask* them, after they're done, what the problem was. You can learn what you *could* have done to further troubleshoot the problem. You might never be an expert at their level, but you can certainly improve a bit. Doing so–even in a system where you might not personally care–improves the overall agility of your mind, and makes you broadly less helpless even when troubleshooting other, unrelated systems.

> Here's another way to think about it: maybe you don't know everything about how a system works internally. Fine. But you can't just say, "I can't do this!" Instead, ask what you *can* do. Sometimes, just in running through what you *can* do in terms of troubleshooting, you'll fix the problem. Sometimes just doing what you *can* do will lead you to a point past your knowledge, but give you enough clues that learning something by watching a YouTube video (or whatever) will get you to a solution.

06. Can Follow the Chain

My friend Jason was recently gifted a small 4-wheel All Terrain Vehicle that was broken. The ATV's former owners simply didn't want to deal with the older machine, and didn't want to spend money (and time) having the local shop look into the problem.

The ATV has an electric starter, which didn't make *any* noise when activated. Jason checked the voltage on the battery and it was dead. However, rather than just replacing the battery, Jason decided to take advantage of the fact that this particular model also has a lawnmower-style pull-start. Still no dice. Well, I guess that's it–might as well trash it for parts, right?

Jason knew to *follow the chain* (pun! The ATV is chain-driven). The pull-starter is a simple device: it's designed to get the motor moving, overcoming the inertia of just sitting still. At the same time, it's supposed to light off the spark plug, which should ignite the fuel in the engine cylinder and get the engine moving on its own. The pull-start moved smoothly, suggesting the motor wasn't frozen up or something crazy. So that leaves two basic root causes to consider: there's no gas in the engine, or the spark plug is dead.

There was certainly gas in the tank, so Jason looked at the fuel line. It wasn't pretty. It seemed pretty deteriorated, and when he detached it, it had a lot of gunk inside. Now, the gunk is too thick to make it into the engine proper, so Jason now had a decent set of possible causes:

1. Bad spark plug. Checking the fuel line didn't eliminate this, and with a dead battery and/or burned-out electric starter, there was no way to test this.
2. Gunked-up fuel line blocking fuel from getting to the carburetor.

3. Gunked-up carburetor blocking fuel from getting into the engine.

At an "Organizational" level, Jason could swap out the spark plug, the fuel line, and the carburetor and probably fix the problem. That's "repair as troubleshooting," though, and it's a little expensive in terms of trying to validate a guess. So he decided to just take the fuel system apart, with the help of a detailed service manual, and clean it all out. He'd replace what he *needed* to, not what he *guessed* was bad.

Jason's not a mechanic. He did have access to a service manual, and he had a basic ability to *follow the chain of problems* and make some educated guesses about where the chain might lead. He had a *little* system knowledge, but certainly not a lot. He might eventually come to a point where he needed more expertise and had to consult someone, but he's equally likely to come to a point where the machine runs again, and he can paint it camouflage with daisies and enjoy riding it through the forest.

07. States Better Theories

A Troubleshooting Mind does not guess. It doesn't say, "well, I think *this* might be broken." I see this *all the time* in my field of information technology.

 "Hey, my computer can't get to the Internet."

"Oh, it might be your browser cache. Try rebooting."

This is not a conversation a Troubleshooting Mind has. This was just a guess; it's something that maybe worked in the past, and so rather than troubleshoot the problem, we're just going to throw spaghetti at the wall to see if it sticks.

A Troubleshooting Mind *states theories*. Theories are things against which you can conduct experiments to see if the theory is correct or not. In the above dialog, *no theory was stated*; a "repair" was attempted to see if the problem would simply go away.

A good theory is *falsifiable*. That is, you can run experiments to both *prove* and *disprove* the theory. **This is a big deal and so I am going to go on about it at some length**, because people just don't get this. But it's huge. Read through the following theories and tell me which ones are, or aren't, very good:

1. There is no electrical power.
2. God does not exist.
3. Batteries are badly designed.
4. The car has no gas.
5. The car has been driven badly.

Theories #1 and #4 are good ones. You can prove, through an experiment or test, that they are correct or incorrect. You can *prove* them, but you can also *disprove* them. They're fairly binary; they are either correct as stated or not correct.

Theories #2, #3, and #5 are not good theories. They cannot be definitively proven, and they cannot be definitively disproven. They're more statements of *opinion*, and opinions have no place in troubleshooting. In troubleshooting, *facts* are what matter.

What about a statement like, "no spaceship has ever landed in New Mexico?" Is it a good statement of a theory? Well, it *is* falsifiable. All you have to do is produce one spaceship, and you've proven the theory false. From a troubleshooting perspective, though, it's not a great statement because it would be *very hard* to prove or disprove it. It's maybe a fine statement for a philosophical debate, but it's not the type of theory we focus on in troubleshooting.

In troubleshooting, it's important to *think* about each theory you form about why something is broken or not working. Make sure each theory can be *proven* or *disproven*. Ask yourself: how would I prove this to be correct? Or, how would I prove this to be incorrect? If you can't think of a way, then you probably don't have a great theory.

08. Brainstorms the Problem Domain

When you encounter a problem, you don't immediately need to start forming theories about what might be wrong. That's especially true for unfamiliar systems. Instead, just grab your notepad and start writing down *anything you think might be wrong*.

My iPad won't turn on.

- Could have a dead battery.
- Could be bricked.

* Screen might be malfunctioning (maybe it's on and you don't know it).

Just write down every possible problem you can think of. Then, start looking at ones where you can form a proper theory. Okay, maybe the problem is the battery–fine. We can test that by plugging it into a known-working charger for an hour or so, to see if anything changes. Of course, that's not really *falsifiable*, because if an hour on the charger doesn't change anything, you still don't know that the battery isn't completely kaput... but it's at least an easily testable theory to start with, and it *can* be disproven if not proven.

Once you're done brainstorming, *save what you wrote down*. This will be hugely useful the next time you're troubleshooting that system. As you gain experience, write down new potential problems you learn about... and you're well on the way toward forming a Knowledge Base!

09. Can Troubleshoot Stuff That's Not Totally Broke

Some of the most frustrating things to troubleshoot are the things that aren't actually broken, but just aren't "acting right." This is especially true when complex systems have some kind of bottleneck, or weak point, that is causing the poor behavior. In these cases, *many* less-experienced troubleshooters will just start grasping at straws, attempting to change every possible thing they can to see if anything "helps." This isn't a good approach, and it can often lead to making the problem worse, or creating all-new problems.

Start by stating a theory: "My car is fine at low speeds, but the engine starts to make odd noises when I speed up. I think the fuel line may not be delivering enough fuel for faster speeds." It's important that your theory state either a possible *cause*, or at least a *condition* you can monitor. In this case, the theory is that the fuel line is not supplying enough fuel.

Next, *try to make the theoretical problem worse*. So, in this example, you might *carefully and professionally* try to make the car go *even faster*, while obviously obeying all laws and being absolutely safe. If going faster makes the problem worse, then you may be on to something. It still might not be the fuel line, but you've at least confirmed that the problem is speed-related. You've built something of a wolf-proof fence; you know that whatever the problem is, it's related to the speed of the car. Ergo, any system that doesn't really change as the car gets faster, like the radio, is no longer suspect.

You do need to be careful, because it's easy to "make things worse" and actually make *multiple* things worse. That doesn't help narrow things down. For example, "my computer is behaving slowly, and I think I might be out of memory." Removing some memory will "make the problem worse," but that's *always* going to be the case. You may have simply introduced a whole new problem that's unrelated to the one you set out to solve. So before you "press down" on some situation to try and "make it worse," make sure you understand all the potential outcomes of what you're about to do.

10. Seeks Commonalities

Humans are marvelous pattern-finders. Sometimes, we actually try too hard to find patterns, and end up thinking things are related that aren't really related. But in troubleshooting, our brains' pattern-finding abilities can be incredibly useful. A Troubleshooting Mind seeks out patterns, and it does that by trying to find commonalities between systems.

 I've divided this territory into two, using a wolf-proof fence. I notice that one side of the fence is pretty much all an icy river, and I don't see a single wolf. I'm going to quickly scan the other icy rivers—nope, no wolves! I think a common trait of icy rivers is that they don't contain wolves. That will speed up my search. I can just ignore the icy rivers.

One big step in troubleshooting, which I've covered already, is that you need to try and replicate the problem you're dealing with.

- Computer can't connect to the Internet? Try another computer.
- Light won't come on in the room? Try a light in another room.
- Debit card didn't work in ATM machine? Try another card.

Each time you run a test against something similarly situated, you eliminate one or more problems with a truly wolf-proof fence.

- The other computer worked. The problem is definitely not with the Internet service.
- The other room didn't work, either. Maybe a circuit breaker is tripped, or power is out to the entire house.

- The other card didn't work, either. Maybe the ATM isn't communicating with the banks.

A Troubleshooting Mind will almost instinctively seek out commonalities; this is one of the first troubleshooting steps that really becomes habitual and almost automatic. ATM card doesn't work? Try another card, or try another machine. You certainly wouldn't march right into the bank and complain without at least trying an alternative, right?

How are these things like each other, and how are the different is a skill built deeply into our brains, and it's one that can serve us well in times of trouble.

11. Is Calm; Projects Calm

The biggest problem with troubleshooting is right there in the name:
Trouble.

Unless it's that Pop-o-Matic board game, trouble isn't fun. It's not something most people look for. It's something we try and avoid. Trouble represents a problem. A failure. Nobody actively wants problems and failures in their lives! And so trouble can make us nervous. It can make us panic. It can make us feel pressure, especially when those around us are feeling fear and panic.

Fear, as the saying goes, *is the mind-killer.* Fear, nervousness, and panic will kill your Troubleshooting Mind. You can't build a wolf-proof fence if you're in imminent fear of the actual wolf jumping out and biting you–your brain just wants to *run away!!!* So you often have to take an active role in calming yourself, and activating your Troubleshooting Mind.

Different people have different ways of doing this. Some will just take a deep breath. I personally tell myself, "you know, I got this. And in a hundred years it won't make any difference anyway." I'll ask those who are panicking near me to take a break and go somewhere else for a bit. I remind myself that I know what I'm doing, and that I have a good methodology. I know how to research, and I have confidence in my ability to learn.

This can be *hard* when someone's really leaning on you about a problem. Try walking into an office where for some reason *nobody can print anything*, and you're the guy responsible for the printers. Everyone is screaming, because *of course* today is the one day when *everything* has to be printed or *the entire world is going to stop spinning and we will all fall off and die!*

Have some stock phrases handy.

Hey, I totally understand how important this is. But I need to be calm, and I need to use my mind, here. I need to follow the troubleshooting process so that I can solve this for you. I can't be running around like a chicken with my head cut off, but you're making me really nervous. Can you give me some space? I promise it's the fastest way to help me solve this.

Get into *your own head* and get yourself into your groove. Follow your methodology. Above all, **do not take shortcuts**. When everyone else is panicking is *especially* the time to not take shortcuts, because too often those shortcuts will cause you to miss something, end up causing you to take longer solving the problem, and increase the level of panic in the room. Be cool. Be calm. Try to project that calm, so that others feel, "hey, he/she has this, and I feel I can trust them. I'll chill out a bit."

Part 3: Storytime

Analogies are great. I love analogies. Properly done, they're a great way to frame something new in a context that's already familiar to someone else. And so that's what this Part will be about: a variety of analogies, or stories, at least some of which I hope will "speak" to you. In them, I'll frame out some of the concepts covered elsewhere in this book, in an attempt to give you more context and real-world applicability.

POP! The Weasley Outlet

I have a cabin up near the Dixie National Forest in Utah, and it's very much a do-it-yourself project. The original structure dates back to the mid-1980s, and it was expanded in the mid-2000s, but much of the building was constructed by the people who owned it and lived in it. As such, almost every project becomes a bit of an adventure.

Case in point: we were using an electric concrete mixer outdoors, and kept losing power to it. It was plugged into a GFCI outlet (yay safety, but man, I hate those things), and sometimes the GFCI would pop. Other times, the circuit breaker would pop. Now, there are obviously a few possible root causes, and so I brainstormed them:

1. The appliance is pulling too much current.
2. The GFCI outlet is getting old, and is popping prematurely.
3. The circuit breaker is bad for some reason.

Of these, one of the easiest things to check is #1, at least in part. I checked the mixer's manual, and it assured me the appliance wouldn't pull more than 8 amps. On a 15 amp circuit, that should have left me plenty of leeway. I'd normally have to start troubleshooting #2 and #3 next, but... that'd be hard. There was definitely another, easier thing I could do before that, which was to connect an ammeter to the mixer. This is basically a clamp that goes around the mixer's electrical wire and plugs into my multimeter, allowing me to measure, in real-time, the amount of electricity being used. I had someone watch the meter while I loaded more concrete into the mixer and turned it on. It went for a bit, and then POP! went the GFCI.

"What was the amps reading?" I asked.

"It was just above 12," I was told. Lying manual! 12 amps should still be well within the circuit's capability, but for an old GFCI outlet it might be just enough to trip it. And it's certainly possible the mixer had previously peaked closer to 15 and tripped the circuit breaker. But popping the GFCI at 12 felt like the most likely root cause, and so I set out to replace the outlet. Actually testing a GFCI outlet requires specialized equipment that I didn't have, so I was definitely engaging in some repair-as-troubleshooting, but I had *some* evidence from the ammeter backing up my decision.

A new GFCI outlet turned out to be just the thing I needed, and we finished up the concrete project in a few hours with no more interruptions.

The moral here is that while the ammeter wasn't going to definitively point out a root cause (unless it spiked above the circuit's 15 amp capacity), it was a simple, cheap, and easy test. It didn't completely divide Siberia in half, but it did carve off a little section, letting me focus on a bit less in terms of possible root causes. When a test is quick, easy, and non-destructive, it doesn't necessary *need* to eliminate exactly half of your root causes. So long as it can eliminate a few–or even implicate something a bit more strongly– it's served its purpose in the troubleshooting process.

It's What You Project

"Hey, Debbie, I got the ticket from the help desk–what's going on with your computer?"

"Emil! Oh, thank God. I don't know–*everything* is gone. My desktop icons are gone. My files are gone. *EVERYTHING* is gone!" *If you can't tell, Debbie is pretty panicked at this point. She was in the middle of month-end closing figures, and it's like her computer reset to factory-new on her.*

"Oh wow. Um, okay–wow. I've never seen this before. Have you tried rebooting it?" *Emil is starting to sweat, because he's really never seen this happen before, and he's picking up on Debbie's panic.*

"Of course I rebooted it! I did it four times! You guys always say that, and I know sometimes it works, so I just did it! But it's not doing *ANYTHING!* Can you get my files back or not?" *Debbie hasn't quite lost it yet, but she's justifiably concerned–this is her job, and it's going to take weeks to redo everything if Emil can't fix it.*

"Um, okay–" *At this point, Emil sits down at Debbie's computer, opens a web browser, and starts using Google to try and search for solutions to the problem.*

"Are you seriously Googling this? Right here? This is how you're going to fix it?" *Debbie is moving past panic and into anger, and it's not hard to understand why. Emil isn't filling her with confidence.* "Can you get anyone else to help on this? Why are you here if you can't help?"

"It's just that all your files might be lost forever, so I wanted to start seeing if there was a way to get them back." *Emil is almost stuttering, and he's not thinking clearly before he speaks.*

"ARE YOU KIDDING ME? GET SOMEONE ELSE HERE RIGHT THIS MINUTE!" Debbie isn't happy.

"Oh, yeah–um, sure." *Emil stands, and is visibly shaken. He doesn't want to go back to his team and look like an idiot, but Debbie's scared him pretty badly.* "I'll go back and get somebody."

"Get someone smart!" *Debbie's lost confidence not only in Emil, but the whole team. The next person is going to have to do a lot of work to regain her trust and to help her calm down so that they can fix the problem.*

"Hey, Debbie, Emil said you needed some help. I got him to explain that your computer seems to have reset and you've lost everything– is there anything more?" *Tom speaks with urgency, but does so calmly. He wants Debbie to know he takes this seriously.*

"Tom, hey, other than losing absolutely everything, no, that's it." *Debbie's pretty sarcastic, and Tom hears the anger in her voice.*

"Okay, I can work on that right now for you. I just wanted to make sure I had the whole picture. I know you've probably rebooted, so we'll skip that. Can you tell me what you were doing when it first went all wrong on you?" *Tom's remaining calm, and he's letting Debbie know that he's not going to force her to go through the usual troubleshooting ringer. He's also gathering more information on the symptoms and scope, which is good troubleshooting.*

"I'd just sat down, and it said it needed to reboot to apply an update. That took half an hour, and it came back like this." *Debbie's calming a bit, because she feels Tom's engaged in solving the problem. She recognizes fact-gathering as a step in the process.*

"Ah, okay. That gives me a good clue, thank you." *Tom sits at the computer.* "I need to log out and log in as myself to troubleshoot this. I don't see any apps open, but just to make sure, you're okay with me logging you out?" *Tom's in the seat, but he's acknowledging that it's still Debbie's computer. He's smart in letting her know that what he's about to do isn't just another reboot, which would likely irritate her.*

"No, it's fine." *Debbie's calming a bit more, because Tom already seems to be taking something she recognizes as an active step in solving the problem.*

"So, just so that you know what's happening, the computer basically keeps all of 'your' stuff in one spot. Everything on the desktop, all your files, even the layout of the app menu, is all in one folder. It can actually store all that for many different people, in case people share a given machine. So I'm just looking at the spot where it keeps all that." *Tom's still logging in, but he's explaining what he's doing. This isn't so much to educate Debbie as to let her know Tom knows how the system works. But it shows Debbie that Tom respects her and her intelligence enough to assume she'll follow along.*

"So my stuff might still be there?" *Debbie's gone from calm to downright hopeful.*

"It's possible. It came up looking like a factory reset, I think, because that's what any new user would see. You're obviously not a new user, but it may have just lost track of something. Yeah, see here, there's two folders with your name. I bet this one with the '-1' is the new one." *Tom's stated a troubleshooting theory, and he's now in the process of testing it.* "Did you have about thirty or so files on your desktop?"

"Yeah, that's probably about right." _Debbie's now peering over his shoulder, completely calm. "Yes! Those are mine!"

"Okay, cool. So nothing's lost. For some reason the update just made a new user account for you, but the old one is still there. I'm going to log out, and I need to go make a couple of changes on the server so it'll reconnect your files with your account. It'll take me about thirty minutes, but you have to stay logged out the whole time. Is that okay?" *Tom's setting an expectation for Debbie on how long this is going to take, and reassuring her that all's well.*

"Sure, is there any chance what you're going to do will delete the files?" *Concern is creeping back into Debbie's voice, because she doesn't understand all the back-end stuff that Tom is about to do.*

"It's pretty remote, but I'm actually going to have the server pull a full backup of your computer first. That's why it'll take so long, but I figured you'd prefer safe over speed." *Again, Tom's trying to be reassuring, and letting Debbie know he's taking her seriously.*

"God, yes. I'll go get a yogurt or something. Just grab me in the lunch room when you're done?" *Debbie's fully calm now, and exhibiting trust in Tom to solve the problem.*

"Absolutely. I'll see you in about half an hour."

Part of being a troubleshooter is often dealing with the people who you're helping. In those situations, *be cool.* You need to *project* calmness as well, because whoever you're helping will likely be in a panic. You don't need to lie and pretend everything is under control if it isn't, but you also don't need to feed into their panic with dire news that isn't yet validated.

If you run into a situation where you're going to have to do more research or tests, you might want to take things "backstage" if you can. Troubleshooting almost always involves some trial-and-error, but it can look like fumbling to someone who isn't familiar with what you're doing. That can lead to a lack of confidence, which means they're less likely to provide good troubleshooting clues to you. Moving "offstage," as Tom did at the end, is a way to be doing something productive, and avoid being seen as "fumbling." For all we know, Tom may have run back to his team screaming, "oh my God, it's all lost forever and we're gonna die!" but he kept his cool in front of Debbie.

The Non-Leaky Hose

Troubleshooting can be tough when whatever you're troubleshooting is totally broken, but at least in that case you're dealing with a fairly static situation. With the thing being broken, at least it's not a moving target. What's even harder are situations where something is working, but not working *well*. One situation where that applies is when you suspect some kind of *bottleneck* is causing poor performance in something, but it's not completely broken.

I was once helping a friend fill a newly resurfaced swimming pool, and it was taking *for eh ver*. It was bad enough that we basically had to rely on one garden hose, which just doesn't carry that much water; on top of it, the hose itself was gently burbling water out like it it had all the time in the world.

Troubleshooting: try to replicate the problem. I got another garden hose and hooked it up to the only other hose bib on the house, which was completely opposite from the pool. Of course, the hose wouldn't reach. We contemplated running to the hardware store for another one, but it was already late in the day and the hardware store was a good distance away. So I tried the other hose where it was, and it *seemed* to produce a pretty strong flow. But... it was hard to tell if it was the hose, the hose bib, or something else.

Troubleshooting: try to state the entire problem domain. Well, the hose could be clogged. The hose bib could have caked-up sediment or something. The house could just have poor water pressure, which you wouldn't necessarily notice at a faucet or shower head, since they often create additional pressure by using internal restrictors. It felt as if the easiest thing to test would be the hose itself.

But how do you test a hose? Well, in cases like this, one trick is to actually take the thing you think is causing the bottleneck, and *make it worse*. If the problem gets commensurately worse, then you've probably put your finger on the problem, and you can work to resolve it. If the problem doesn't get worse, then the problem is probably somewhere else. So I stepped on the hose a bit. No change– the water continued to burble out. I unhooked the hose from the hose bib–we hadn't done this before because, frankly, it was in a really awkward position and all but welded on from caked-up calcium deposits (I have really hard water where I live). The end of the hose looked fine, but the hose bib looked a mess. I turned it on, with no hose attached, and sure enough–burble, gurgle, not woosh-swoosh. The hose bib was toast, and it was soldered on, so it's need a real plumber to fix it.

The bib on the other side didn't look nearly as bad, though, so we connected our two hoses together, and they *just* reached the pool. We turned on the second bib, and the water came out *much* more rapidly. So much so that the water pressure inside the house dropped noticeably, which we regarded as a good thing.

I realize this wasn't an earth-shaking situation, but it's a simple example of how a bottleneck works. Most systems have several points where performance could be impeded, and each of those carries varying degrees of difficulty in terms of troubleshooting. Picking one and *making it worse*, so you *know* where one bottleneck lies, is one way to test them. When I bottlenecked the hose on purpose, and the situation didn't get worse, I strongly suspected the hose wasn't to blame; it wasn't carrying anywhere near its capacity, and so my artificial bottleneck didn't make the problem any worse. That forced me to look elsewhere for the problem, which we eventually found.

The Leaky Network Server

When I was at Bell Atlantic Network Integration in the late 1990s, I helped migrate us from the NetWare 2.x operating system to the Windows NT Server 4.0 operating system. We made this migration pretty invisible to users through a piece of Microsoft software called File and Print Services for NetWare (FPNW). Basically, it made a Windows server "look like" a NetWare server, and so all the computers in the office continued to work without modification. The server also supported a dozen or so printers. Now, NetWare and Windows work a bit differently with printing. With NetWare, the printer is "smart," and basically has its own user account on the server. The server holds on to files that are waiting to be printed, and the printer periodically logs in, checks for new files, and prints any that it finds. We migrated the dozen or so printers to the Windows technique, where the printer basically just sits there, and when the server has something to print, it reaches out and tells the printer what to do.

Everything was pretty smooth for the first week, I'd guess. Then the server crashed and shut down. There's no easy way to troubleshoot that in a lot of cases; we rebooted it, turned on a lot of logging to try and catch it if it happened again, and went about our business. About three days later, it crashed again. Perplexed, and seeing nothing unusual in the server logs, we asked ourselves, "what changed?" Remember, that's not troubleshooting. We were kind of unsure how to troubleshoot the problem, though, and so we figured if we could identify a change of some kind, that might lead us to a root cause. Almost like clockwork, now, the server was crashing every three days. Eventually, we gave up and just restored the server from a backup that had been taken right after the migration. This was essentially the answer to the "what changed" question–now, we knew that *nothing* had changed, since the server was exactly as it was when it was first activated.

Three days later, it crashed.

We were out of clues, and so we paid to open a support ticket with Microsoft. We arranged for one of their developers to basically dial into the server using high-end diagnostic tools, so they could "watch" the server "under the hood" and see what was happening.

The problem, it turns out, had been the printers. Or rather, the printers had exposed an underlying problem. We'd never de-configured the printers from behaving in the NetWare fashion, meaning they were still trying to log into the server to get files. They were *also* waiting, Windows-style, for the server to send files over, but the printers were perfectly happy to engage in *both* behaviors. Each time a printer logged in–and each one was trying about every three seconds–the FPNW software would allocate a small chunk of memory to deal with the login. But when the login *failed*, it wouldn't deallocate all of that memory. Instead of releasing it all back to the operating system, a tiny bit of memory would get "lost" with each failed login. After about three days, the server would "run out" of memory and crash. The fix was twofold: we deactivated "NetWare" mode on the printers, and Microsoft issued a patch that corrected the "memory leak." There's even an archived Microsoft Knowledge Base article about it[1].

So, problem solved, but only after a lot of time and angst. And you know what? *The clue had been there for us all along.* We went so quickly to "what changed?" That we didn't use all of the tools available to us. While the *server* log hadn't shown anything, the *security* log was full of "failed logon" attempts: one per printer about every three seconds. If we'd noticed that, we could have disabled "NetWare mode" sooner, and while the underlying problem wouldn't have been fixed, we would have prevented it from

---

[1] https://jeffpar.github.io/kbarchive/kb/179/Q179995/

cropping up in our environment.

That's why I tend to think of "what changed?" as a crutch, and while I don't regard it as proper troubleshooting. I'm not saying it's never useful, and sometimes it's the only thing you can do–but think *really hard* about whether it is in fact the only thing you can do, before you jump to it.

The Water Heater

This is a good story of troubleshooting a system you know nothing about.

I have a cabin up near the Dixie National Forest in Utah. Like many homes, it's got a hot water heater. Like many cabins in the area, this one's hot water heater was *old*. Like, probably 12 years. The water in the area is iron-rich to say the least, and even with filters, it puts a lot of wear on a water heater. And also like many cabins in the area, we shut it down entirely for the winter (I hate snow), meaning we cut off the water supply, open low-level cold and hot water drains, and so on. We try to empty as much water as possible to avoid a burst pipe. Because the electricity is a little iffy in the winter, and because the water heater is electric, we shut off and drain as much water as possible from it as part of shutdown.

And then Spring arrives! We make our first trip to the cabin, close the low-level drains (or have our own private Bellagio fountain show), close the water heater drain valve, and open the main water supply. We bleed the air from the lines throughout the cabin by opening each faucet until the water runs steady. I then cut the water heater's circuit breaker back on, and we go about our opening procedures.

An hour or so later... no hot water. Huh. Well, that's not totally unusual. We'd discovered in a previous year that each of the two heater elements had its own little plastic circuit breaker pop-button thing, so I trundled to the basement to pop 'em back in. No sizzling noise, like you could usually faintly hear as the heaters kicked in. An hour later, no hot water.

Uh oh. This was on top of a caved-in skylight, by the way, so we were really sweating our chances. And I know *zip* about hot water heater repair. But, I mean, how *hard* can it be? It's electricity going to a couple of things that're pretty much what you'd have on an electric stove, right?

So I downloaded the thing's manual, which had a section on troubleshooting. First step, check the breaker. Done. Second step, check the voltage on the elements using a multimeter. Easy. 220v all the way. Third step, shut the circuit breaker off and check the resistance across the element, using the same multimeter. Infinite resistance–the element was burned out.

This is not, apparently, an unusual problem, because Home Depot sells a Hot Water Heater Repair Kit containing two new elements and a thermostat. While Loving Spouse drives down the mountain to buy one, I start re-draining the heater, after shutting off its water inlet valve on top. When the new Kit arrives, we unscrew the old water heater element and

 This portion of the story has been removed due to the extremely profane language used.

the water was gushing out at us! "Holy

 Sorry, more profanity.

, get a bucket!" I'd *just* drained the damn thing, where was all this water coming from? Well, it was sure draining fast now through the 2" hole in the side where the element used to go. Oh, and the element didn't come out. Not all of it. What came out was a 2" long stub, while the ones in the new Kit were like 8" long. The stub was all corroded. Hmm.

So we did the bucket brigade until the water got below the level of the hole. Now, at this point, you *have* to do some logical thinking.

1. If the top element was corroded, odds are the bottom one is, too. This must be why the Kit comes with two of them.
2. If this tank is still full of water, then the drain valve in the bottom is probably clogged with goo and corroded metal parts, so it never really drained.
3. We need a new water heater.
4. We can't get a new heater now, and it's nighttime, and we need a shower. A hot one, this time, with less cussing.

Buckets at the ready, we removed the lower element. This one was bad, but not as bad; I'm guessing the bottom one only comes on if the water is really cold and you're using it fast, kind of as a backup to the top one. More bucket-ing. Install two new elements. Open water inlet valve

 Profanity. Sorry.

just tighten the elements down!!!" Okay, no leaks. Now, at this point, again, some logic:

1. Water is coming in the top.
2. Water should flow naturally to the bottom, because gravity.
3. Top is full with air with nowhere to go, which is going to compress as the water enters.
4. At some point, the compressed air may be strong enough to prevent new water from coming in. I know our water pressure is about 50psi, and it doesn't take much to get air to 50psi.
5. If I turn this thing back on and both elements aren't underwater, they may explode or something. It can't be good.
6. I need to let the air out the top.

I don't *know* these things, but I strongly suspect them, and logic would suggest that I'm right. Now maybe the air isn't ever going to get to 50psi or so and stop the water from coming in, but it feels risky.

Flashlight in hand, I poke around the top of the heater until I see what is very obviously a pressure-release valve. That is, it's a valve, and it's on the top of the tank. It's not there for good looks. I open it, and air commences rushing out. Water is going to soon follow it; I get a bucket ready. Sure enough, water starts spurting out. I close the valve. The heater is full of water. Circuit breaker on... and *success*. I hear The Sizzle, and a bit later we enjoy a nice shower.

And a couple of days later, we replace the heater. This time, we get an old pool cleaning host and a big funnel to catch the water and route it to the basement drain, because removing the elements is the only way to get enough water out to lift the damn thing off its base.

The point here is that *I'd never done this before.* I still don't know a lot about the inner workings of a water heater, although I'm imagining now that they're less magical than I'd suspected. I got a manual, followed some basic steps, watched a YouTube video on using the multimeter to take the measurements, and *figured it out.* I also learned a good bit about caring for the new water heater so that this doesn't happen again. I stuck with *logic*. I followed a procedure. I *thought about why* I was doing these things, and used those facts to draw conclusions. That's the Troubleshooting Mind. Even wet.

Electrifying!

Sometimes, the *obvious* problem isn't actually the problem, it's just a symptom.

I'm not an electrician. I'm also not a plumber, roofer, framer, or concrete-er. But I do co-own a cabin up near Duck Creek Village in Southern Utah, which is a remarkably contractor-free zone, so you learn to do things yourself. Like the outlet in our former snowmobile garage (I don't do snow, so we made it into a gym) that kept going out.

Now look, we all know what the problem likely is when an outlet is out, right? If it's a non-GFCI outlet, then something probably tripped the breaker. I've used that example previously in this book. If it's a GFCI outlet, then probably the little GFCI button is popped. In this case, it was a non-GFCI outlet, and sure enough, the breaker was tripped. Fine. Reset the breaker, all's well. It was likely just a momentary overlo–

BAM. Tripped again.

What a second, *I didn't even plug anything into it!* Okay, maybe something else is overloading the circuit, but it's something that cycles on and off like a space heater or something. Fine. I'm following a methodical process here, right? So I leave the breaker off and go find everything else that's seemed to lose power. I unplug *everything.* Reset the breaker. Fine! Now it stays on. So I can just plugging in one thing at a–

BAM.

What the *heck?* There is nothing plugged in! Okay, the Troubleshooting Mind really goes into overdrive now. Electricity is scary, but it isn't actually complicated. The wire comes from the breaker, and goes from outlet to outlet to outlet until it reaches the last outlet. If nothing plugged *into* an outlet is causing the problem, then it may be the *outlet itself.* Now, I can't see the wiring, so I don't know what order the outlets are wired, so I just start pulling them out of the wall. As I do, I "short" the wires together with wire nuts, so that it's basically a continuous circuit with the outlet removed. After each removal, I flip the breaker back on. BAM, BAM, BAM. I remove the last outlet...

And the breaker stays on!

Joy, happiness. But I'm a little tired now, so I don't start putting the outlets back in, although I do toss that last one in the trash. I go upstairs for a glass of water and–

BAM.

What. The. Actual. Heck.

Okay, follow the chain. Be logical. What is actually *in* the circuit at this point? The breaker and a bunch of wire. Well, it's not like wire "breaks and overloads the circuit!" It's just wire. So the breaker must be bad. Hoo-boy, that's a pain to swap out, though. So I'm standing in the gym next to where the last outlet was, contemplating pulling the entire breaker panel apart.

Scritch, scritch. There's a noise *in the wall.*

In. The. Wall.

Yeah, I'll spare you the gory details at this point, but a *mouse* got into the wall *and chewed the wires.* Which was actually fine when he wasn't *in there moving around,* because when he moved around, the now-exposed wires would touch, spark, short out, and trip the breaker. This was also, obviously, a huge fire hazard, and I could see the scorch marks on the wiring and the insulation. So the end problem was a spot where the wall covering hadn't been properly applied, and a mouse (well, a family, really) had gotten into the wall and decided to snack on wires.

You see, *follow the chain* is a really important thing to do. I was making this big assumptions that wires were the least fallible portion of the system, when in fact they were the proximate cause of the problem (aside from mice). Needless to say, a good deal of work ensued, from replacing the wires (I cut out the damaged section, installed a junction box in the wall, and spliced the wires inside the box) to replacing the wall and all those outlets.

The moral, though, is that the problem you *see* may just be a symptom. To truly *solve* something, you need to follow the chain from one end to the other, and make sure that you actually fixed the *problem.*

Spoiled

When you've worked on a given system long enough, you tend to get a feel for what tends to break, and that lets you focus your troubleshooting efforts. But it's also easy to start taking shortcuts, which means that when something less-usual breaks, you end up spending a lot more time troubleshooting that would have really been necessary. My solution? *Documentation.*

Take the time when I was working on aircraft. This one particular model had little flaps on the top of the wings called *spoilers*, which would raise and partially killed the lift on that wing. That would the airplane to kind of "lean" to that side, which helped the pilot turn, by *rolling*, left and right. These flaps were connected to little hydraulic actuators that would push them up and retract them. The actuators themselves were all connected to a long steel rod. That enabled all of the actuators to work in unison (nowadays, it's all done electronically, but this was a 1960s-era machine).

When you assembled the system, you were supposed to run it and make sure that, with the rod all the way in one direction, the spoilers moving edge would recess just slightly below the rest of the wing. All the way the other direction, of course, the spoilers would pop almost straight up. When everything didn't line up, troubleshooting it was almost always easy: the rod was just misaligned. You turned a couple of nuts a quarter-turn and tried again. In fact, that's not even troubleshooting, it's just *assuming* the problem and fixing it. That worked so well, so often, that I almost never even looked at the maintenance manual, which clearly outlined a troubleshooting procedure.

Well, one time, twisting those nuts didn't solve the problem, and I probably spend most of a day fussing with that damn thing. The more-experienced mechanic I was working with wisely let me waste the time, so that I'd feel the pain of what I was doing wrong. In the end, I got the manual, followed the actual troubleshooting procedures, and discovered that one of the actuators was actually not working correctly, and it was putting strain on the control rod, which prevented the other actuators from working correctly.

The moral here is to *document a consistent troubleshooting sequence* and then *always follow it*. This doesn't mean you can't optimize: if there's a particular cause that *usually* causes problems, troubleshoot that first, every single time. But actually *troubleshoot* it, meaning *prove that a fix is needed* before just twisting the nut and making a fix. And as you learn more about a system, you an modify your troubleshooting sequence. Perhaps you discover a test that can more definitively eliminate several possible causes all at once–add that to the list in the appropriate spot. But *always* follow the same sequence of troubleshooting. It saves time, and it helps make sure you don't miss anything important.

What Could it Be?

Here's a story that literally just happened to me–I'm actually writing this right after the fact. It hopefully demonstrates a few aspects of the Troubleshooting Mind, especially in less-than-tranquil circumstances.

My company is based on Salt Lake City, but I live in Las Vegas. I needed to go up to SLC for a few days, and coincidentally had recently gotten a new car that I really wanted to take out on the road. So I made the roughly 6-hour drive to SLC, spent a few days, and drove home on a Friday morning.

Roughly halfway through the trip, I decided to pull over, top off the gas, have a bio-break, and grab a bite to eat. *Just* as I'm pulling off the exit, the car chimes, warning me that the tire pressure in two tires is low. *Uh-oh.* I'm not, like, in the middle of civilization at this point. There's a gas station, a McDonald's, and not much else. The car helpfully informs me that I can probably continue on, at speeds under 60MPH (ugh!), for some time if I need to. My inner troubleshooter immediately kicks in: what could possibly be wrong?

I'm not some kind of automotive expert, but tires are also not that complex. Because I'm not an expert, I decided to start running through a list of everything that could possibly be wrong that I could think of.

- Tire puncture
- Some kind of other leak, like around the stem valve
- Faulty tire pressure sensor
- Tires were never properly inflated to begin with
- Slashed tires

Now, the car's already told me that *two* tires are bad, so by the time I get parked in front of a coin-operated air pump, I'm already tentatively building a wolf-proof fence to eliminate the things that are *deeply unlikely* to occur to two tires at once:

- ~~Tire puncture~~
- ~~Some kind of other leak, like around the stem valve~~
- Faulty tire pressure sensor
- Tires were never properly inflated to begin with
- Slashed tires

Logically, I can eliminate another because I've already been driving for around three hours, and I don't recall any James Bond-style sequences where someone jumped on the car at 85MPH and slashed two tires without me noticing:

- ~~Tire puncture~~
- ~~Some kind of other leak, like around the stem valve~~
- Faulty tire pressure sensor
- Tires were never properly inflated to begin with
- ~~Slashed tires~~

I park, and call up the car's status screen on its computer (yay, in-car computers!). It shows the exact same tire pressure of 32PSI in both front tires, which it's flagged in orange, and the exact pressure of 36PSI in both rear tires, which are green. I open the driver's side door and look for the tire inflation label. It says the fronts should be at around 38PSI, and the rears at 41PSI. So either *all four* pressure sensors are bad, or:

- ~~Tire puncture~~
- ~~Some kind of other leak, like around the stem valve~~
- ~~Faulty tire pressure sensor~~
- Tires were never properly inflated to begin with

- ~~Slashed tires~~

Of the entire problem domain I've listed, this seems to be the most likely cause. The tires were *evenly* inflated, just not to the proper pressure. It's likely that this, the first long-haul burn-in, revealed the "barely sufficient" nature of the dealer's inflation work. I topped everything up as best as possible–gas station pumps don't have the most accurate gauges—and waited a few minutes for the car to register the change. Everything was at least 38PSI, and flagged in green, so I decided to continue.

And made it home safely, obviously, since I'm typing this.

The point here is that I took a moment, even just in my head, to list the *entire* problem domain. That gave me a kind of checklist to work against. Why bother? Well, because some of those things had factors in common, like, "deeply unlikely to occur to two tires at once," which let me at least tentatively "wall them off" and consider other possible causes. That list let me form and test theories more quickly, which led to a faster resolution. Believe me, on a 99-degree (Fahrenheit) day, "faster" was really nice.

In Closing

Well, that's it. Hopefully, you've now got some confidence that you *can* troubleshoot like a pro–even if you're not one. It just takes some patience, and above all else, a solid commitment to a *methodology*.

Good luck!

www.ingramcontent.com/pod-product-compliance
Lightning Source LLC
LaVergne TN
LVHW051709050326
832903LV00032B/4105